donpelliott

Chic

From
"The Soul"

A Collection of Thoughts

By

Don P. Elliott

Soul Asylum
Poetry and Publishing

To Sonia
Hugs & Love
Don
4-20 2000

Note for Librarians: a cataloguing record for this book that includes Dewey Decimal Classification and US Library of Congress numbers is available from the Library and Archives of Canada. The complete
cataloguing record can be obtained from their online database at:
www.collectionscanada.ca/amicus/index-e.html
ISBN 978-0-9784909-9-7

Published in Canada by Soul Asylum Poetry
79 De La Salle Blvd, Jackson's Point, ON L0E 1L0
www.soulasylumpoetry.com

Cover Art Design: Charles Ross
Project Editor: Kenneth William Cowle

Soul Asylum
Poetry and Publishing

10 9 8 7 6 5 4 3 2 1

"My Words and Thoughts...Forward"

It has been years and a great deal of apprehension to finally come forward with all that I have written. It has been my only Friend at times...my Healing...my Heart's craving...my Spirit and Soul...and most...my Humbling. When I write it can be thoughts or feelings from within, the beyond and from those I have come to know through my Life's Journey. Some "Scratches" I have been requested to write and the others are my eternal Hopes and Dreams of what I can only wish could be for ones close and or me. I am truly in awe of the many stories, the emotions and feelings of the very many I have chanced to meet over the years. Perhaps a message, a meaning...possibly a gift or a curse...I will not relinquish them? Are some of these messages from beyond or of the subliminal mind? This is the one question that will always remain unanswered. Maybe I will never know as long as I am of Flesh and Blood and of this our planet Earth? If what I have written touches but only one single Spirit or Soul...I am honored and have exclusively fulfilled my chosen Destiny...thus I give you my Chicken Scratch ... From "The Soul".

"Be Safe...Be Good To You...Stay Inspired"
Don P. Elliott

Acknowledgements

I would not have the ability to sustain this Heart, Soul and Spirit if not for the Love of my Mom and Dad, my three amazing sons (Ryan, Justin and Brandon), my wonderful daughter-in-law Jennifer and my two most precious grandchildren Victoria Elizabeth and Dylan Thomas. I would be amiss not to include my once Life partner and best friend Cynthia for an incredible journey through a life thusfar that will never be forgotten, nor one of regret. To so many family and friends that shared in the music, the laughter, the joys and the tears…I am blessed for such a profound Legacy and Family Heritage. To all my Cousins and especially to the ones that once called me "Outer Limits"…I Love you all dearly for giving me strength, respect and dignity…remember…what goes around…comes around…cheers. And last…but certainly not least for such incredible Love, Inspiration and Spiritual guidance…my Heart and Soul always and forever… "Just Me".

Dedications

To dedicate this first book of "Scratches" to so many would be virtually impossible...if I have missed you...I have not forgotten you...okay maybe temporarily...I'll call it memory loss and aging for lack of better words.

~To Those Beyond~

My Mom...Muriel Jean, Grampa and Nannie Elliott, Grampa and Nannie Davis, Uncle Merile, Aunt Doris, Uncle Harlan, Aunt Irene, Uncle Bill, Beverly and lastly Rick Scott.

~To Those Present~

Kim, Tom, Gary 36, Nonnie, Gregory Lee and David Fitz, Alyssa, Emma, Carol, Denise, Linda Lou, Sarah, Shelley, Karen, Gerard, David, Erin, Chrissy, Twyla, Eileen, Gail and to those I have yet to meet...I will be truly honored and blessed when the time comes.

Always Me...Hugs and Love
Don P. Elliott

"Love"

Love has no Boundaries…
…But only if the past has been set Free
For Love cannot be sustained in Fear…
…But to die in silence, that is inevitable

"Greatness"

Strive for Greatness and you will always be the best that you can be…

Never expect to receive Love, Health or Wealth and you will never be heartbroken…

"Friendship"
(For Wendy)

Is it in dreams we see the visions of all that is to come?
Is it in fear that we hide and wait, in Love entranced by none?
How to cover the ground once lost, to endlessly follow the Sun
To cower and shun from darkened days, for whom has really won?

Reach within to find these fears and banish them from your Soul
If be it through fear and darkness, a heart weakened takes it's toll
Just ask my friend, I will find a path and clear it of every stone
In honor I will guide you, you shall never walk alone

In distance I will be near you, in closeness I will be afar
Never to alter or sway your Spirit…to let you be just who you are
So go forth my friend, dare to dream, fear not what has yet begun
For "Friendship" has no boundaries…when two unite as one

"Special"

"Special" is not nearly enough to describe what you mean to me,
Your presence your thoughts, your kindness were always meant to be.
From the moment you were born, your Spirit would begin,
To cast and shape the future, to keep you from all sin.

And as you flourished and blossomed, to the person you are today,
So many you have touched...with your warmth along the way...
Perhaps not many speak of how your amity became so dear,
But it is only when in absence, they only wish that you were near.

No I cannot tell you enough...of just how "Special" you are to me,
Your friendship awards me hope and strength,
to be the best that I can be.
So I leave you with my thought for this day...
deep from within my heart,
Without you there would only be endings,
without you there could be no start.

"If I Were The Moon"

"If I Were The Moon" and you the stars
Would you surround me still?
Could you shine brightly for me each night
Should darkness weaken my will?

Could you shine throughout the night
When all we thought once lost?
Could you find a way to return once more?
In time or place, what would be the cost?

These are questions, I have no answers
I ask of you now and then
A simple assurance, a test of strength
My only reason to shine on again

"If I Were The Moon" and you the stars
I would shine for you each night
To warm your Heart, to brighten your Soul.
Never far…never far from your sight

This and more I can only imagine
As another day surrenders to night
You are the stars that give me hope
In my heart you will always bring light

"Tomorrow"

*Let today be a stepping stone that leads to "Tomorrow",
And carry as you go only happiness, not sorrow.
For in each and every moment you will find what is good,
And given time and patience, yesterdays reasons now understood.*

*In each day begins a path, a path we've never known,
And only should you ask or wish, you will never walk alone.
Yes, I will walk beside you; my hand is yours in need,
I'll listen and give you hope, to be your true friend indeed.*

*So let us take "Tomorrow" and let us leave this day behind,
Tomorrow is a new day; too hope one further gentle and kind.
And if it is not what we wished for, do not carry a heavy heart,
Everyday will bring new meaning, everyday another place to start.*

"My Friend, My Daughter"

As you look upon this day in years to come,
Look at it as not an ending, but a new beginning.
You are and hold the future of all that is good,
What you say and what you do is only what you wish.

So many are proud of what you have become,
It only seems like yesterday that you were so fragile.
But you have grown into a beautiful flower,
I am proud to Love you, "My Friend...My Daughter"

Reach out to find all that you are and can be,
There are no mountains you cannot climb.
Yes, I will be there for every step you take,
Not to lead or follow, but beside you when you ask.

This is your day to once more celebrate life,
Your accomplishments, take pride in which you are.
My Love is unconditional, yesterday, today and tomorrow.
My Pride, My Life, "My Friend...My Daughter"

"My Mother…My Angel"
~ Muriel Jean Elliott ~

I am weary…weary of being all that I could be and more
I will forever regret what I must soon leave behind
Rest eludes me…my heart aches…and yet yearns to explore
A time beyond all of this…a time further placid and kind

I have been cast out from one life…only to begin another
Did I choose to see this to the end…yes, of your will?
One day I will see its fruition…you as my guide…
"My Mother"
You are here beside me…since you have gone…always…still

When all seemed lost…my world became elusive of Love
It was you that again inspired hope, faith…to again believe
To forgive…to forget…to look far beyond and above
To give all of my Heart to some that would in time deceive

The years I denied myself of your presence…I am humble
Not a moment ever passes that I do not look up to you
You have been my guardian…to catch me when I stumble
Never to let me fall…but to lift me up…to always be true

My Love for you is without end…I wish you near me
I dream to embrace you, to hold you again…my reason to live
To envision all you wish me to see…all you wish me to be
You gave me my life…not to aimlessly squander…but to give

I am truly blessed…I will honor you always…
My Love without end…"My Mother…My Angel"

"Touched By An Angel"

*Angels need lots of Love
Because they give so much away
In our need they come in silence
Throughout both night and day*

*So many shapes and sizes
No barriers, ethnicity or creed
Remember to never deny them
For it would deter their destined need*

*To share their gift of Love
To guide and lead us on our way
To bring us healing and happiness
A bring us light to our darkened days*

*Once touched you'll feel their Spirit
A warmth so Soulful, so Deep from within
It is yours, may you share it with others
Yes, it is here your journey begins*

*To travel another road in Life
A gift from Heaven and the Stars above
Their eternal message of Hope and Spirit
But most of all too share that Love*

*For it is you....you were chosen to be...
"Touched By An Angel"*

"The Spirit"

I often wonder where life would lead
Can't imagine now, without you
A sorrowed heart, a ravaged Soul
Now touched by a Spirit so true
From where you came,
I need not ask nor question what lies before me
To instill the light, my life once dark,
These eyes awake, now open to see
In silence you came, no remorse you healed
I am humbled beyond compare
You sheltered me in the depths of your Soul,
As the Dragon steals away to it's lair
To teach what once thought vanished in time,
Lessons of the Spirit so long overdue
I am so gracious you embraced my Soul;
My heart yours, always forever and true
Our journey begins; I will take your hand;
Ever so gently down the road to tomorrow
Yes, I will follow and stay the course,
Together from the past we abandon all sorrow
No longer captive to the hands of time,
Let us travel a distance far and beyond the sky
If this our time to be all and more,
Never a valley too deep nor' ever a mountain too high
No longer I will question where life will lead,
I won't imagine not ever without you
A contented heart, a newborn Soul,
Each day blessed by a Spirit so kindred…so true
From where you came,
I am honored in the presence of the Life and Love you give me
No longer we walk alone, never again captive by time,
To Love and Be…we are Free...

"The Calling"

I have felt your presence profound within me
At first you seemed distant…perhaps my denial?
An entity I soon would feel…I soon could see
Words…a gift or curse…to bring about tears…a smile

To inspire and instill faith…to make ones believe
Simple words from a kindred Spirit and Soul
In each a message…to hope…to find truth…never to deceive
So many years in lament…now alive…now so whole

I am only but a child to all that I have learned
A renewed empathy…beyond the facade…to peer inside
"The Calling"…I am sanctified…unaware I have yearned
No longer captive to silence…too share…too never again hide

To whom or those I bestow my jubilation…my reward
My promise to never deny you when you have spoken
I will pen your message…to honor you with no discord
To never refute "The Calling"…the circle will remain unbroken

"The Beggar"

He sits silently on the street corner
Just another so called "annoyance" to passers by
Nobody knows his name…no one seems to care
He does no harm…he quietly says "Hello"

A voice so meek, so timid…perhaps afraid to cry?
His slightly twisted body…his hands shaking…acceptance?
Perhaps pride from the years before hold him back?
Hold him back from being angry, bitter…afraid to speak?

I am sure there are many stories he could tell
A lost love, a family, a career written in stone?
Tossed to the wolves by society and corporate philosophies
Only he knows…pray tell that someone would care or ask

Why do we fear human kind…why the silence?
Do we feel shunned and sickened by what is deemed the lesser?
Are they…do they not fit society's harsh but yet pristine mold?
Are we right to judge…to abolish…who are we…hypocrisy?

Our so called "Free World"…ignorance driven
High priced prostitution of greed, the monetary and the material
The politics of the "Common Man…Woman"
We take all for granted, to believe that it could never be us
…but could it..??

He sits silently on the street corner
Just another so called "annoyance" to passers by
Nobody knows his name…no one seems to care
He does no harm…he quietly says "Hello"

"Virginia Tech"

A Prayer and Dedication to The Fallen and Their Families…

For I have done no wrong...

but today I have paid the ultimate price

But onward goes my Spirit...

my Soul yours to cease all unrest

Should my demise lessen all anger and pain...

I accept this sacrifice

For the many I leave behind...

I ask Lord, from this my Soul…my Spirit

…may they be Blessed

"The Dancer"

She reaches down to gently caress the leather wings that adorn her feet
Adjusting ever so carefully the binds that embrace her legs…anticipation
Becoming one with the melody…her mood…rhyme and element…they meet
Reaching out to welcome the Heavens…inviting Angels to join in her elation

Her movement precision…the matured wooden planks commit to memory
Remembering her every pace…her engagements…breathing life into Dance
Tribal is her rhythm…the Spirit of Life invades her Soul…captive in harmony
Expressions from beyond…from deep within…her Heart, her Soul in trance

She reaches down to gently caress the leather wings that adorn her feet
Adjusting ever so carefully the binds that embrace her legs…anticipation
Becoming one with the melody…her mood…rhyme and element…they meet
Reaching out to welcome the Heavens…inviting Angels to join in her elation

She evolves…she becomes…"The Dancer"

"The Past...The Future"

Life ripples through the water...another reflection soon to fade
For we are the only true bearers of the choices we have made
Look not in sadness...should those colors turn to Grey
Look for only happiness...tomorrow dawns another day
Keep your dreams alive...too behold, too gently nurture
Bury only what is deemed the past...but bury not the Future

"Our Destiny"

Perhaps what seems at times a lifetime away...
"Believe"...these are the moments to seek joy in the reflections…
…Joy in the Spirits that came before us...now passed...
Where we have been...what we have accomplished...take pride...
Where tomorrow will lead us, we need not ask nor question....
Live to be all that we can for those that warm our Hearts...
…For those that fulfill the voids in our Souls...
Our Family....our friends..."Believe" and it shall be...
That my dear friend is and will always be….
"Our destiny"....

"For Cindy"
~ My First Poem For You ~

Can it be a miracle…my dreams come true?
Fulfilling every fantasy…finding you?

Hair of gold and amber…your beauty Maiden fair
So precious like the sunlight…created with special care

And now that I have found you…one thing I can't deny
Your Love has given me wings of strength so again that I may fly

And always we'll be together…for our Hearts unite as one
Our Love is our's forever…Bonded by the Son

I Will Love You Always and Forever Without End…

"Cynthia"

On this one of so many days I've looked back with fondness
I look back to the times when the World seemed like Ours
Ours to build and create, Ours when time seemed endless
Oh, how the years go by, how quickly they pass, minutes to hours

Of all this time, I could not have traveled
to the places I have seen
Experienced and envisioned the dreams
that came from your heart
The loving embrace of your arms,
now in remorse of what I have been
My World now hurt and angered,
Our World now so distant and apart

To say so many words in such little time
could never in life replace?
The many hours you have given to those
we Love without me there
Of all I could have been, I wasn't,
if only in time these I could erase
I would be the fool to believe
that time is kind to those in despair

So I am left humbled and with
only these few simple words to share
You will always be in this Heart and Soul...
a Love I deem without end
Not to relish in all that
I have done so wrong, but to say I truly care
I say the words "I Love You", these words until death
I will honor and defend

Love Always...
Don

"Always There"

The deep of the morning is upon me
No, not even the darkness is awake
Thinking of you, to wish again of what can be
To be with you again, to reach inside but not to take

I did not come to Beg, Steal or Borrow
I reached inside you too give comfort…to heal
To remind and instill, I will be here tomorrow
To share from my Heart and Soul…what is real

I believe in not only you, but also in me
I believe in what lies beyond the darkness
Beyond all sadness and tears…if only we can be
Our chance to be all…too love…hold and caress

Our strengths lie in not one, but us as two
Our unfulfilled Dreams, ours to build upon
To share and believe, as I always believe in you
Hold me thru this darkness, Dream with me until dawn

Let us not relinquish this our moment
The moment we have to Love and Share
Our Hearts and Souls alive…again with content
Never alone will we be, together always…
…"Always There"

"My Friends"
21-11-56

Gaze towards the Heavens one star struck night
And choose the one star that shines so bright.
Though surrounded by so many, never to confuse,
This star dawns a light it shall never lose.
And no matter how far or distant it may seem,
Like that star I will shine for your every dream.
So whatever your wish, or wildest fantasy,
This star is yours, and shall always be.

21-11-07

I am…because it is my Destiny…
My trials…my tribulations…once only a mere path
A path that now bestows a value greater than any treasure
A Journey obsessed of my Spirit and Soul
To seek truth in myself…to be true to others
To believe in Faith…Hope and Love…
It will be….

"I Am Who I Am"

" I Am Who I Am"
Do not try to change me
It is I that must do that
Except me from what lies within
Not from the outside
I am simple, natural, a Spirit
Constantly looking inside
I must believe in me
I will not set goals I cannot attain
I will dream in reality
Not beyond what is certainty or real
I must be content to be whole
For it is sorrow that weakens one's Soul
Look for truth, nothing less
And all will be right.
" I Am Who I Am"

"The Writer"

The morning is brisk and airy as it leisurely awakens...
the dawn of a new day
The fire red sun levitates slowly
to gently warm and embrace its young
All is calm...not a sound...solitude...alone...
my mind adrift, far and away
To another place and time it travels...
one I have longed...my heart unsung

I hurry up only to wait...
the anguish and impatience of where I yearn
I have much yet left to do here...
many chapters to close...many to release
My age is golden...seasoned...
my only torment is time...I await my turn
My inner voice cries out soon...
to be distant from the broken dreams...at Peace

The promise of my Spirit...
it will not deny me that time nor that place
"Instill hope and faith in your expression...
share them...embellish your dreams"
My Sprit is constant...to encourage...
to hasten yet deliberate my pace
A pace meticulous...calculated...not crass...
not always what it seems

Soon to return...where the Land meets the Sea...
where time is without end
A land anointed by the Heavens...
Angel laden stars consume the darkness of night
My home...far and away...a chance to grow...
to be whole...to heal...to mend
The words that drive my desire, my passion..
I am "The Writer"...I will Write..

"Metamorphosis"

Like the changing of the Seasons…mine is upon me
The past…the many years wrought in both anguish and elation
Now a veteran of so much…belated…inevitable…to be
Darkness no longer seeks my presence…my release…illumination

Like the dawning of the new day…I awake to my senses within
I see and feel so much I had never thought possible…it is real
I feel the want…the determination to Love…to conclude…to begin
Patience and time has been my only friend…a time to heal

To expose what has been veiled for so long…no longer the illusion
To assent this heart, no longer cloaked, dormant…
to Love without fear
No longer will deception lie in wait…to unmask the confusion
To transit the limits I have known for so long…my time…
my time is here

I am complete…I am whole once more… "Metamorphosis"

"Silence"

It is now cold where warmth once gave residence…once content
The heavens enthused by ambiguous phantasms…uneasy
Disconcerted…these currents once tranquil aroused by "Silence"
A "Silence" unrequited will soon expose those lost in duplicity

Vanquished dreams take on a lurid face of disillusion…ill fated
The gifted who patiently awaited this reunion…
now tense in elation
A calling long overdue…now becomes loyal to free will…release
Sent from beyond…no longer a wrath…
but inspired from revelation

Those who shamed certainty…soon will be shrouded in sorrow
Unable to oppose what only in time would reveal with vengeance
The disguise of both night and day will not shelter them…it is time
In haste they arrive…to right what is wrong…to avenge the
"Silence"

"Time"

What is Time when we choose silence over being heard?
The Time we spend living for only regrets
Living for the broken dreams we hold so near
Our visions and hopes of what should be
Are we wrong to believe and wish for all?
If Time is borrowed, what is the cost?
What is the cost of indecisiveness?
What is the cost of hindsight…perhaps our demise?
Time is too Precious; to take it for granted…such a loss
Live, Love and Laugh…Time is on our side when we share it
If not borrowed but shared…there is no cost for fulfillment
Treat Time as if there is no tomorrow
Tomorrow is but another day for one's so fortunate
Time is but a Moment…but only a Moment In Time

"The Gift"

Often I question why we met
Why we found in each other a want, a need
To satisfy our tormented Hearts and Souls
To taunt and challenge who and what we are
To question our Past, to welcome our Future
Was it in our destiny to only come this far?
To unite as one when all seemed lost?
Perhaps we need not question our Path, our Journey
To accept what was and what will be
So many doors remain unopened; we are "The Gift"
"The Gift" that only two can share as one
What we give, we give without question…without remorse
Our paths may or may never cross again
But we will take and remember always what was given
Only in time will we truly understand the meaning
The true meaning of "The Gift"

"The Reason"

*Lost in a World she could never understand
Too afraid to let go of the pain, of the past
She guarded her Heart and Soul with a Velvet Steel Hand
Never to be given, not without a dire fight to the last*

*Her demons that lie in waiting, they await their prey
Awaiting ones that would attempt to break down the wall
And as the wall was broken to dawn new light, a new day
Again they would surface…another they craved…soon to fall*

*But one would remain steadfast…destined to heal
To be there…to abolish the pain…the past
Never to be anything more than true…to be real
To be more than those that came before…perhaps the last*

*A journey long but destined to be what could only be so right
"The Reason" …neither would or could ever truly understand
And as they shared…the light changed from dim to bright
Together in unison…to cease all hatred…pain…
she reached for his hand*

"Alone"

Alone in her determined distance
from the world she once knew
The unknown…her new found companion…
her only friend?
She remembers a time when many were near her…
now but a few
She questions their reasons, her being…
did she scorn or offend?

She asks…where did they go…why did they leave…
how could this be?
Abandoned, confused…an austere reality,
her trials and tribulations
Her loneliness utters only silence…
afraid to believe again…afraid to see
Would time heal what became her unconscious f
all from grace…desolation?

Her beliefs scattered like the autumn leaves…
no direction…so surreal
The many colors she had worn…to appease others…
but never for her
She collects her reason once more…
to reveal only solace…to again feel
Her only empathy must come from within…
so afraid…so unsure

Alone, resolute to prevail over, to find what and who is true
To seek new conviction…unbridled her course…
to believe once more
For those that had passed her by…
that deceived her…their intent askew
No longer captive, Alone…to journey from the past…
to fly again…to soar

"If"

If sorry is the hardest word I say…
I will say it one more time
If letting you know I believe in you
I will say it forever in rhyme

If I dry your tears and give you strength
I will be your rock…your solid ground
If allowing you time to think things through
I'll encourage silence…I'll utter no sound

If hopes and dreams are what you wish
I will see them through in your light
If holding you close to make you feel
I will Love You Forever…our eternal night

If words are never enough to declare
Reach inside me…my Heart…this Soul
If ever in times we quarrel in anger
I will respect you…my solitary goal

If ever you think I could love another
My heart is yours…it will never be sold
If only one wish be granted in my life
"Love Forever Ours"…as we grow old

"The Journeyman"

She sits consumed by the numbing silence…
in awe of his ingenuous words
The truth that she had so longed to hear…
now a burden…her forsaken desire?
A past captivated by lies and cunning…
timid her cries…at last finally heard
Embers that burned measured and meticulous…
now erupt by his passion…his fire

His quest to bring her warmth…
to bring luster to a light that had grown so frail
To believe…to heal…but only thru patience and time…
born from what is true
Could fear bring upon her self imposed destruction
once more…her consent to fail?
Only she could amend what the past had scoured…
to begin…to start anew

His words she could not be denied of…
but to ascend from his steadfast compassion
To breathe life…to infuse truth where lies
were once resident to the unknown
"The Journeyman"…from a darkness
he once induced…sincerity…now his only vision
If only for her to trust in his words…
to foster all the empathy he had shown

How long would he continue beside her…
would he grow tired and weary of uncertainty?
He would not force her hand…
but only instill hope in what lay beyond her sorrow
A gift of hope…a rise of faith…to believe in truth…
life no longer seized by disloyalty
Had she found the inspiration she had awaited so long…
her answers to tomorrow?
…in him she would find…"The Journeyman"

"Colors"

Show me the "Colors" that you dream in so I will dream them too.
I long to feel your every thought, to be a part of you.

In every waking hour, my heart entranced by you.
But as the night grows near, this heart lies cold yet true.

No, I cannot change the way we are, or what we have become.
But my promise to love you more each day, until my life is done.

I ask for nothing in return, except for this I pray.
That love will lead us to our place, to bond us there one day.

Show me the "Colors" that you dream in, so we may dream as two.
Of a place where rainbows touch the Heavens, a place for me and you.

"Shed No Tears..."

*"Shed no tears" for me my love
For I have not gone far.
Your needs, desires, a warming voice
I'll come to where you are.*

*For you my love are special
You are my call from grace.
You have found my inner spirit
One I thought I could not replace.*

*My friend, my heart, my love
I plead your beckon call.
Should ever their come a moment
That you should stumble or fall.*

*My arms my love will hold you,
To warm, to comfort and care.
To brush a tear from your sad eyes
And to softly caress your hair.*

*No, "Shed no tears" for me my love
For I will not be far.
Your needs, desires, a warming voice
I will come to where you are.*

"The Things I Miss"

When I look into your eyes I see the beauty
Of all "The Things I Miss"
The warmth, the love and compassion
A heart changed by just one kiss
In you I have found the strength again
To battle for a dream once lost
As rivers and water run ever so deep
You built a bridge so that I may cross

From this I can offer you little
For I am a simple man
In return a piece of my heart each day
Given time you will understand
For you are so very special to me
No, not no one can replace
It is you that has awakened this lonely heart
That of endless time will never erase

"The One"

He remembers how they came to meet, not so very long ago
In her he found true meaning, their love…destined to grow
He often stopped to wonder as he caught her gentle glance
Could this be something more, or fate intended to chance

His heart was his and only his…for this he would control
Determined to never be dispirited…his past had left a hole
He remembers how she touched him, compassion in her heart
She taught him of all that matters, could this be his new start?

And as he looks before him, these things he'd always miss
That day they spent together, how her touch became a kiss
Could this be just a beginning to a road with many bends?
Their pain, their love, their passion, would there ever be an end?

In this he took for granted, the pain she felt within
The many times she would open the door…only to let him in
Weakened by her loneliness, her heart would soon grow cold
But he would hold the truth inside, his heart remained untold

In loss she found new meaning, in strength her turn to grow
For him was this "The One" true love, why did he let her go?
Perhaps too late to change the course or question what had become?
For in his heart now lies the truth, she would forever be "The One"

"Don't Be Afraid"

*It is not only about Love when I reach deep Inside You
But to comfort and dry your tears, to mend your heart so true
To learn, to share, trying to understand the joy or pain you feel
It is in you my Friend and Love I find…not Illusion but what is real*

*Each day and every night, my only wish is that you will be okay
That again we awaken to tomorrow, no not to me just another Day
But another chance or moment to be, to be again with you once more
Too many years I too have feared, afraid to step…to go beyond the door*

*"Don't Be Afraid" to share the pain, "Don't Be Afraid"to cry
"Don't Be Afraid" to speak the truth, "Don't Be Afraid"to try
To Love and share comes from within, be it joy or pain we feel
I am here my Friend, my Love, my Life, no…not Illusion, I am real*

"Parallel Lines"

Two lines run side by side along the sands of time,
Parallel or similar, but yet so diverse in many ways.
To complement, to synchronize, in time destined to meet,
But time has not been kind as they struggle through their days.

Alone, feverishly striving to reach their final destination,
If only together could they be, no, not a distance too great.
A life, long in patience…disenchantment soon takes its toll,
No, time has not been caring as they hasten only to wait.

To persevere the elements, the Earth, Fire, Wind and Water,
With no remorse they come in readiness, to erode what was the past.
But sacred remain the ties, one day soon these lines will convene,
To bond, together in unison, the final journey lies before them…at last.

"Full Moon"

I steadied my weary eyes, gazed deeply into this Moon,
To find it full in darkness, luminescent on weakened Souls.
A mask of foolish games prey on those with hearts so kind,
Why do you bring about pasts, the ones thought long behind?

Oh yes, you are deceiving, cunning and quick to consume,
You uncover every weakness, you unlock infallible doors.
Your presence I cannot relish, overwhelming is your light,
I sometimes wish for blindness,
then forever beyond your sight.

The nights that lead to your coming, sleepless, deep in trance,
The days you hide with passion,
knowing again another chance.
Again, once more this Soul is yours,
as your wish I have no will,
Be placid to one's I Love my plea,
this heart lay cold and still.

Cease the torment, abolish their pain,
please take me as the one,
To let others live without hatred, unjudged and free to choose.
To choose and have no boundaries, to Love without remorse,
Allow them destiny, a future,
from their hearts with no recourse.

My plea, my passion, and yes,
once more without reason nor rhyme,
Your shroud of mystery and darkness,
why to others and I so unkind?
I will cease to breathe and exist in your presence;
will you take me now forever?
Per chance then and only then, this
"Soul" becomes tame with contentment?

Again, I steadied my weary eyes,
looked away to avoid your gazing stare,
I need not see you to be embodied by the pain
and darkness you bestow.
My eyes need not be open to see visions of what lies before me,
I am angered, saddened and lost, and of all,
in your presence I am beaten.

"Eclipse"

*Had he been here before…he pondered the question?
A thought, a dream, a lyric…a message from beyond?
Only now to realize its fruition…to become full circle
Oh, the tormenting Moon and the power it beholds
Capturing those too weak to deny its captivating glare
Eclipsed to darkness and then to light…
in that moment it steals
Steals away from those, all that was gained…
only to begin again
Powerless they scurry and run without sense or direction
He challenges the Moon and its power…take me, try
I have been here before, I will not fall prey to your game
He begs, pleas for mercy on those too weak to know
Be kind, leave in haste and set their Souls free…
Please let them be…please let them go*

"The Wind"

The Wind lay still as a whisper, in slumber it patiently waits
Not one can predict its power…its unrelenting torrent
The gifts it can bestow…but yield to unrepentant traits
To seethe destruction, to renew…to seek solace or torment?

I have been The Wind…I have succumbed to its wrath
My direction void of intent…latent, covert in disguise
I am remorseful to some that have crossed my path
To others I prove no mercy…their prying…their own demise

I can be as warming as a heartbeat…yet bitter as the frost
To bring inspiration and lifting currents to those who are in need
Cursed to those lacking virtues…those deceitful and lost
My constitution is strong…determined, willing to serve indeed

I seek no vengeance…only justice as deemed by those above
Only a messenger…the bearer of tidings…the good and the bad
To renew one's Spirit…release one's Soul…instill Life…to Love
To bring about renaissance…to inspire meaning in all that they had

The wind lay still as a whisper, in slumber it patiently waits
Not one can predict its power…its unrelenting torrent
The gifts it can bestow…but yield to unrepentant traits
To seethe destruction, to renew…to seek solace or torment?
…"The Wind"

"The Journey"

The road that I have recently traveled
A distance I never thought possible
"The Journey" I had thought endless, without a meaning
My shoes worn to the "Soul"...
by humbling and deep emotion

My feet are weary, but my Heart, Soul and Spirit reborn
I do not wish for anyone to walk in these shoes
Be true to each and every moment in Life
Be loyal with unbridled dedication and conviction

Be it your dreams, visions...the ones you Love
Do not become stealth and distant with resentment
Find your Spirit and let it guide you
And if you are true, it will never stray you or part

"The Journey" is not a rhyme, but a reason
An awakening to those possibly lost, in despair
Be strong and steadfast should it be yours to take
Have the will to succeed, you will overcome and conquer

No, not alone...look upwards and beyond this World
It is of those that have passed before us...their legacy
Fear them not...it is in their Spirit to be yours
To be there without your expectations...your guide
Your destiny as in mine... "The Journey"

"The Path..."

As I peer down the path that leads to tomorrow
I feel the humbling, a weary heart and mind
It is a feeling of warmth, yet cold and helpless
To remind us of the past, a road so unkind

But I will not be frightened by illusion and deception
As always it is only what I wish or deem to believe
I have courage and strength as I beckon to my Soul
For it will not stray or wrong me, nor shall it deceive

I am here for a purpose, to uncover the unknown
To heal and to comfort both the strong and the weak
To free all vanquished Souls, no more torment and sorrow
To allow the deaf to listen, to encourage the quiet to speak

To Live, Laugh and Love with all one's heart can bear
To fill one's world with hope, to teach one how to care
No, I will not be broken or strayed from my life's quest
For it is in my destiny, for all who wish to share

So, I go now to tomorrow, with an open heart and mind
To take what lies before me, no deception, no despair
The secret of my journey, this simple gift called "Love"
The Love from one that is true, the one that is always there

"The Door"

*The Door to his destiny was left open once more,
How many times would he and did he try to close it?
The question always remained…what lay ahead…the open door,
A gift unopened…a question in time to finally be answered.*

*His heavy heart…a darkened Soul,
The hurt, the pain, the anger now tempered to perfection.
So very few would understand what lay deep within,
Only those that left the door ajar were chosen to know.*

*The few that went beyond the veil to bear their Heart and Soul,
One day he would return…the closing of the door.
Destiny would prevail…the truth unmasked…the naked Soul,
The past now the present…the truth behind the unknown.*

"The Awakening"

Another sleepless night, awakened by the dawn
Silence fills the room, lonely dark shadows abound
The memory runs deep of when I last looked upon
A Soul like no other, not another will ever be found

Relentlessly the reminder of a touch so gentle and true
A loss, another's gain, and happiness her longing reward
Free to face the world, her weakness, to believe and do
To conquer and overcome, let no one place discord

Now I must take my place where destiny has chose
A place, not a distance too far…where I may lay my head
Rebirth, this body…this Spirit, like the seedling to a Rose
I awaken to sounds of the Sea, her memory is my bed

Tormented by only a dream, the memory now fading fast
So real yet always illusion, why does it hurt me so?
For I have done no wrong, why do you tease and never last?
Until the day I do not awaken, come that day I will finally know.

"I Sleep Alone"
(For Paula)

*The many nights I lay wondering…
Where would I be…what could I be?
Some surround me with torment…
Some with desire…what I only choose to see
The nights are my canvas…
I put my life into visions and dreams
I become one with my expression…
My Heart, Soul and Spirit drive me…
Not what it seems…
Others often wonder who I am…
What I seek…am I different?
I feel them explore me…
What are my wants and needs…
Do I wish to be more?
No, accept me…
I am the colors and hues of both day and night
The seeds I have sewn…
I am my own colors and canvas…
"I Sleep Alone"*

"Fetal"

I am the Life that the Ascendancy beyond has chosen to create
I am one of flesh and blood, they encompass my Soul
I am the Spirit of the many lives that came before me
I am born unto a World of torment and unrest
But there is still Love…Hope…Belief…
Do I dare to escape this domicile I have come to know?
Such Love, warmth…sustenance?
This, it is my time as destiny has chosen…I will be
I will not fear the light of day after the quiescence and darkness
I will allow the hands of time to coddle and nurture my Soul
I will allow the Love of my Mother and Father to lead me
…when all seems vanished…uncertain
And time will be caring and permit me to be all that is written
In Life…to be for others
I will exhale new life into unborn Souls…
Nurture their Bodies, their Spirits as predestined
And when the cycle has reached fruition…I will return
I will return in Spirit to the warmth
The warmth I have since longed for a life time
I have returned…I am "Fetal"…my Journey absolute

"Victoria Elizabeth Elliott"

*You are the sunshine "Little Princess" that brightens our day
An Angel sent from above...so much to learn and to share
Yours eyes of Baby Blue...with one look you get your way
A Gift from Love...to be one of compassion...to truly care*

*This is only a small part of what we see...but most...such Heart
Instilled from two loving parents so proud...a present to behold
"Mimo" and "Papa"...your expressions...so innocent...so smart
You bring us Life...watching as you grow...
we can no longer be "Old"*

*You always shine so brightly in our Hearts...
in those you've yet to know
To be young again...no longer our wish...why...
then perhaps never you?
So our "Little Princess"...shine on into tomorrow,
to love, learn, to grow
Bring your light to others...
let them share in a Heart so very warm and true*

We Love You "Little Princess"

"Mimo and Papa Elliott"

"Dylan Thomas Elliott"
April 26th, 2008
10:44 A.M.

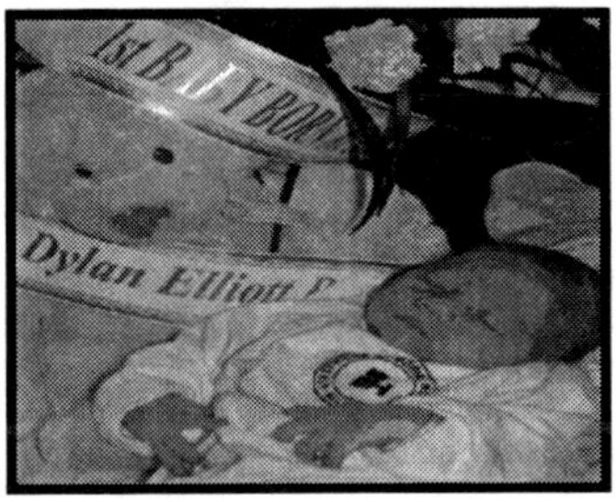

The constellations opened to welcome your arrival…
salutations laden with pride
The stars that carried you to us…yours to continue on the
journey…to sustain you
Heralded only by true love that bode your creation…
sadness and joy…tears I cried
I will know you soon…until then…remember…
"I Love You" …this…my heart true

"Dylan Thomas"…your name emblematic…perhaps a sign…
your destiny in rhyme?
Bear your name with pride…seek out immensity…
yet be humble in your own rite
Let your Mother, Father…your family nourish Love…
wings that embrace you thru time
I will know you soon…until then…remember…
"I Love You" … my will…my insight

When time consents…I will be with you…and when I leave…
take with you a part of me
Remember what we had shared…knowing that there is another
day…another moment
My pride in you will always lift me high "Dylan Thomas"…
beyond delight I will always be
I will know you soon…until then…remember…
"I Love You" … my gift…my present

"Dad"
~ September 22nd, 2007 ~

It is hard to believe how quickly time has passed
As I look back with so much fondness…upon my memories
I am so grateful for all that you have given to us
As your Son, I am so very proud of whom you are

You have been my best friend…
my mentor from my very first breath
I sat so patiently in the wings to hopefully
one day soon be you
But I knew somehow I would never attain
that wish and dream
I need not even try…No, not one could ever take your place

It is you "Dad"…your Love, your Compassion…why we care
So much because of you…
I am humbled beyond words…expression
The joy you have inspired in us all…
the generations that follow
The music you brought to our Souls,
deep from within your Heart

To make us Dance, Sing, to Laugh and Cry…Our Family
Not a day can ever pass that I will not look up to you
The "Ace" of Hearts…The "Ace" of all suits
You wear them like no other…A gift Heaven sent from above

As your Son…and of those that have passed along your way
These few simple and heartfelt words
that stand the test of time…

"We Love You "Ace"…Always And Forever"

Happy 75th Birthday Dad…
…Thank You for Always being "You"

"Thank you"

I "Thank You" for the way you are
...for all you have become
I "Thank You" for sincerity
...your love unmatched by none

I "Thank You" for the time you give
...to ones less fortunate than you
I "Thank You" for your gentle touch
...your heart so warm and true

I "Thank You" for the love you show
...in one's life none could compare
But of all these things I cherish most
...it is knowing that you are there.

"My Friend"

*To take from you and leave
You know is not my style
For you I'll go the distance
I'll travel and endless mile*

*In you I've found the chosen one
For truth you will be my guide
No longer will I feel the darkness
No longer will I hide*

*Let me feel your hunger
Let me feel your pain
Let me feel your happiness
Too surrender all disdain*

*And all I ask of you
My dear, my precious friend
Please allow me the honor
To be until the end*

*Your strength and your weakness
Your night unto the day
Take my hand, I'll lead you
When you have lost your way*

*Let me feel your anger
Let me feel your pain
Let me cleanse your wounds
I will be your healing rain*

"Erin"

In name you are the child of peace,
The one who heals all anger.
To make ones world a better place,
In this you are no stranger.

For you are a gift…too behold on high,
In this your Mother's pride.
Your love, compassion and caring,
These traits you shall never hide.

Your wishes and dreams are precious,
In these hold them near to your heart.
Never lose sight of who you are,
For every ending always brings a new start.

Take pride in what you have become,
On this your special day.
To friends you bring new meaning,
In their hearts you will always stay.

"Happy Birthday Erin"

"Eagles"

*The "Eagles" that we share signify strength from within
In these lay the groundwork from where we must begin
For these we shall hold sacred…always near to our hearts
In happiness…in sorrow…or in times when we are apart*

*Our silent tranquil moments, we soar above the rest
To learn as each day passes, to strive…to be our best
In times of life's uncertainty, touch its golden wing
Questions once unanswered, new guidance it will bring*

*In these we find the power to take on each new day
No, it shall never let us down…nor ever fall astray
Believe in the power, but of all…do believe in you
These "Eagles" share a strength…not of one…but of two*

"The Kiss"

Would we ever imagine years ago of what would be one day?
How a simple Kiss could turn to love, to touch us in so many ways
For me it only seems like yesterday when I stood at your front door
To ask of you that favor, never thinking I could ask for more

For you have taken me oh so far, so many places I have never been
The many feelings, the many emotions, without you I had never seen
I am blessed by every waking moment, in how you touched my Soul
Without you, my life without meaning, this heart could not be whole

So I give to you my Love and pledge that never will there be a day
That I will not only think of you, but Love you more in every way
My gift is simple; a heart weary at times…yet very warm and true
I will Love You now, Always and Forever
…for you there is nothing I would not do

"A Heartbeat"

It only takes "A Heartbeat" to fall in love they say
Yet seems like an eternity…to turn, to walk away
For this I have no reason, except for this I fear
Without you my life is forsaken, my path again unclear
If it be in absence that makes one reach within
To find a deeper meaning, it is here we must begin

And should it be from anger or forces we've not known
If left to walk in prejudice, or left to feel alone
No I will not be far my Love; I await your silent call
If ever you should need me, if ever you should fall
Yes, I will lift you up once more and brush away all fears
To mend your wounded heart, to gently dry your tears

My heart lay still with patience, destiny is my only guide
No, I will not bow to weakness, I will never run and hide
So go now, find tomorrow, to find truth that lies within
True Love is unconditional; True Love is never a sin
And should there be a place for me deep within your heart
Just ask and this I will promise, never again will we be apart

"Fear"

Love is not a feeling or words
It is a conquest beyond any dream
A need, a want, a touch, a thought
So superficial, not what one would seem

Love is two Souls and Spirits, finally as one
As each life had passed, their time was near
Their moment in time, was it destined to be?
So many pasts, so much love, so much fear

Could this be an ending without a beginning?
Only they had the power, only they could know
So little time to find what would lie beyond
So late in life, could this true love grow?

For this the only question, only as two they share
And as each new day beckons, perhaps it is near?
To seek out and find the love, if only they should dare
A love without an ending, a love stronger than "Fear"

"I Love You"

So often she would tell him
"I Love You"…"I Want You So"
Words from beyond her heart
She only wished for him to know

But he would not accept or take
Her words and her faith so dear
So now they remain unspoken
To say them again would only bring fear

A hole he had left deep inside her
Would the pain by no means subside?
And soon might there be a day
She could say and no longer hide?

Words from beyond her heart once more
"I Love You"… "I Want You So"
Yes, she would find the one to accept
One man who would let her know

"I'll accept your words in honor"
"No please, don't run or hide"
"I Too Love You and Want You So"
"My Love For You Shall Never Subside"

"A Message In The Sand"

Worlds apart, yet so close today
Two Souls die searching to find their way
Many times they offered to give of each their hand
But all that they had given…
"A Message In The Sand"

They loved like no other…like none had loved before
And only Two as One…would they find the door
To overcome their fears…to take their only chance
If only he would ask of her…ask of a lifelong dance

A life devoid of boundaries…would be such a joy
To bring back the freedom, he once knew as a boy
But many of Life's trials…lay between his and her hand
They both wrote the words "I Love You"
"A Message In The Sand"

"Reflections 1"

As the water runs by me
The Reflections of my past
Calming like your gentle touch
If only it would last
For this is my world
My own, my sacred place
To be at peace and harmony
To seize the sadness from my face
If only you were here
To share in what I dream
If only you were here
To sit and watch the stream
Yes, you would feel it too
Just what I feel inside
This Love that grows without ending
This Love I cannot hide

"Reflections 2"

I gaze into the water
And see you there beside me
I turn to touch your flowing hair
But illusion again denies me
My heart beats loud and hard
Only wishing you were near
I cry inside, I miss you
I prayed that you would hear
But perhaps it is not to be
This quiet and solemn day
Maybe it will be tomorrow
Your heart will find the way

"Reflections 3"

I opened the door to let him in
Such a fool I must have been
To take your love for granted
If only these eyes had seen
I walked away in silence
Never did I think of such a cost
Afraid and fearing loneliness
How could I ever be so lost?
To throw away the things I love
Of all…this my greatest sin
But second to all that has become
I should never have let him in

"The Angel"

Never a frown or a sad moment my friend
....What was is what was...what is, is what matters.....
Healing comes with time, time is healing....
My faith in you never falters, never for one moment...
Nor has it ever lost its sheen.....I take it every where I go.....
We may not be what we thought...
but we can be what we want.....
A friend beyond a friend.... An Angel sent from Above…

"The Land And The Sea"

You awake to the silence of the morning
The scent of the sea overwhelms your senses
At peace finally, all is quiet, all is calm
You are home; the land welcomes you with open arms

No, not a dream, No, not an illusion
But a reality that takes your breath away
Why did you wait so long it asks?
Where have you been?

Yes, finally home to where you belong
The sand damp and warm, yet soothing to weary feet
The water cleanses your Heart and Soul
You sense you have been here before...but when?

"Who was I, where have I been" you ask?
No, it does not matter, you are home
A Soul once again fulfilled, regeneration now begins
It is what you have longed for, waited for...

You are again "One"
...one with "The Land And The Sea"...

"I Am Home"

The sun spreads it's warmth upon the crystalline water
The genesis of another day, reborn, refreshed and so new
Sounds of silence only hours before have awakened from sleep
The ground now cleansed, glistens from the fresh morning dew

The water grows ever stronger like a heartbeat as it caresses the shore
Slowly inching its way toward the land as if to possess and again hold
But soon it will become weary
and make its way back from where it came
So strong, so beautiful and mystifying, the many stories it has told

Birds of the sea slowly circle, singing…resonating like laughter
As if to boast and brag of who will be the first to catch their prey
They sashay with so little effort, forever at the mercy of the wind
In child like fashion they dive and turn, it's a ritual they love to play

He feels the wind and the sea salt mist caress against his face
Oh, the memories of so many times before, an illusion it would seem
His eyes slowly open, he struggles to focus, amazed…in disbelief
"I Am Home?" "It wasn't just an illusion, no, not another dream"

"Lighthouses"

She would love her Lighthouses
And he would love the sea,
From sadness they found each other
Always together they would be.

But healing would not mend so quickly
Two hearts that had been broken,
His hand would write the feelings
He found so hard to be spoken.

She touched him like no other
When he looked into her eyes,
But pleasures of the world
Would be his one demise.

The feelings he held inside
Not even she would understand,
His weaknesses and strengths
Would be of his own hand.

So onward he would sail
To another port of call,
So easy to drift away
When he could have had it all.

He would feel the constant pain
And forever feel the sorrow,
For the love that he had lost
Would not be there tomorrow.

Now often he will sit
On the banks of the riverside,
If only he had his time back
Would he still run and hide?

These questions he would ponder
As the years would come and go,
Would she still have loved him dearly?
If he had only let her know.

"Us"

Words can never reveal the way that I feel
Nor can they speak for this Soul
A Love deeper than words or expression
Deepness only we two can share

So hard to understand the meaning
But I feel it now like no other
A want, a need, an addiction
Why me, why "Us" I ask?

Our bond, so complete, so Spiritual
A power beyond wildest dreams
Subconscious beyond human imagination
Beyond flesh, blood and bone

I cherish our bond and who we are
To whom or what created this union
I owe my body and Soul
I am finally reborn, I am blessed

Two abandoned Souls finally as one
So right, so real, such rewards
In all of the Universe there can be no other
I am truly blessed by You

"Answers"

If only I had the "Answers"
I would give them all to you
And if only granted just one wish
I would make your dreams come true

Yes, you have been my heartbeat
For an eternity, so it seems
You were my only vision
When I didn't have a dream

For this and so much more
I can only offer you this
My Heart, my Soul, my Love
Without you I would be amiss

So I leave you with one simple verse
That comes from beyond this heart
Without you there could only be endings
Without you there could be no start

"Lost"

I look to the skies for answers
Never really knowing why
Perhaps it is just a reminder
Of when I look into your eyes

I see the pain that I have caused
How could I never see?
Of all the world, and what you gave
I often ask, "Why Me?"

To say "I Love You" now...
And of how you touched my heart
My every day...my every night
My only reason...why I must start

I am sorry of what I have come to be
If only I had known
How it could break your honest heart
If only I had shown

My Love so true if only sooner
Might have saved this troubled Soul
But now this heart lies lifeless
A Love lost has left its hole

To change our destiny and what we dream
Oh! At such a cost
It is only until it is too late
Two hearts yearn for what is "Lost"

"Afraid"

"Afraid" of being who we are
At times so hard to bear
"Afraid" to look inside our hearts
"Afraid" to show we care

"Afraid" to reach out for the hand
When lost or in despair
"Afraid" to say "I Love You"
"Afraid" you'll not be there

"Afraid" that life will pass us by
Should we hide from circumstance?
"Afraid" of no tomorrow
Because in fear we missed the chance

"Afraid" of being alone again
Yet "Afraid" to start anew
Of all I fear, I fear this most
Is living any moments without you

"Til' The End Of Time"

Let us share for a moment these thoughts for tomorrow
Let us reflect on the happiness and not on all of our sorrow
Had there never been us two, let us not imagine what was lost
Had we not shared this union, what would have been our cost?

We have given of our strengths…exposed our weakness of two
But of all we have shared, we shared a Love strong…a Love true
Perhaps it was in our destiny and over time we are sure to know
That as each new day passes; perhaps again our Love will grow?

Neither time nor distance can erase you…
from this weary heart and mind
It is you I will carry along with me, a Love I will never leave behind
And in what we want of each other, in Spirit we will know just when
It is then we will be complete once more…
our time to reign again

And should that time be nearer in need, no, never surrender in fear
But hold onto what lay within your heart,
look to the stars…I'll soon be near
And everyday I will think of you,
I will dream and whisper in rhyme
"I Love You, Yes, I Love You"… Always…Forever…
"Til The End Of Time"

"Destiny"
Roda & Mike

Today brings our two hearts and these our two Souls together
As it was in our "Destiny" that we have on this day become one
Our future now lays before us, each day ours anew to begin
From each one dawns another, another memory, another done

And only was it yesterday, our lives so different and worlds apart
Now ours to share, the laughter, the tears, to love and to learn
This is our "Destiny"; together we will overcome and believe
Believe in Love, Friendship, patient like the tides to each its turn

May our differences be enough to compliment, as these we will share
To strengthen what each has not, to keep us together along the way
Let music and spirit fill our hearts with joy, may it be and last forever
As it was in our "Destiny", we unite and guide our future this…
… "Our Day"

"When You Were Small"

I often sit and wonder, to imagine "When You Were Small"
The kind of friend I could only wish,
the one I'd stand beside through all
To think of all those years ago, if only to have had that chance
To know and feel the love you share, to feel the joy of a lifelong dance

But oh so sad that would not be,
this man's dream only in time to fulfill
To find you there a gift from high, from that day my heart stood still
An Angel's caress, alluring eyes, hair of amber…a true maiden fair
You would touch me like no other, to show love,
such comfort…such care

As will would be you gave the meaning…
of what Love could always be
To brush the darkness from these eyes,
to dry my tears so that I would see
To see the world in a whole new light, to color what had once been grey
To take my hand…to lead me through…through each and every day

You are my friend, my wishes and dreams…
No, I could not want for more
But if one more wish I would ask of you...
let me be there to open the door
The door that leads to tomorrow, a day of Peace and Serenity
A day that also brings endless Love in the way you had dreamed it to be

No, I need not sit and wonder…
No, not imagine "When You Were Small"
In you I have found more than friendship…
Yes, so much more…I have found it all

"The Meaning"

To seek The Meaning…to reach within
At times…so powerless…so hopeless
Never fear what is destiny…where to begin
To never overcome…to conquer becomes sadness

You are all and more should you desire and believe
Let those who befriend you be your reflection
Like a mirror, those true will not lie or deceive
In each other we find The Meaning…a new direction

I will not stray you…not at any minute or hour
I will not force your hand, nor make your choice
I will be your sweetness should life become sour
I will lead you through the silence…always your voice

"Thoughts"

We are One of endless strength if we Love in Honesty
And that Love shall eternally bind us as One should we accept
We are two if allowed to think and be without prejudice
And as two unite, becomes endless strength to abolish the unjust
We are feeble to believe we have no fear of what lies in tomorrow
For fear of tomorrow can be triumphed when shared with another
A Man is not a Man without the Faithful Love of a Woman
Only a Fool of a Man would foster this loneliness should he not believe
As the fruits of another tree may look, feel and taste so delicious
Don't be deceived by such taste and beauty, as they too may turn sour
Life is to be enjoyed and shared, not alone enhanced by one's greed
I am not alone when you are near, it is you that dawns the light
You are the light and path I have chosen to take until my end
Without you I am empty, only a Soul without meaning…without a dream

"Sullen Is The Man"

"Sullen is the Man" who held all in the World
Shaken is the hand that pens the spoken word
Searching deep inside…to find the lasting truth
Afraid and in denial…no longer in his youth

These and so much more, he hides deep within
Broken are the promises, where must one begin?
Two Souls again run lost, just like their time before
From room to room they'd run, never to find a door

Where does it end he asks, this fear and this pain?
Without her he is lost, at times he feels insane
A road many times traveled, they know they've been before
If this must be an ending, why can't there be more?

Who would levy such judgment, stand now in my sight
Who gave you the freedom, who gave you the right?
To take the love we thought…so righteous and so true
So few would truly understand, so few that really knew

As water may run deep, so will it be our bond
Perhaps one day we will find our world…one that lies beyond
Until that time I will not be still, nor will I lie down and sleep
My Soul is yours my friend; it is yours alone to keep

"Faith, Hope, Love"

This moment in our time I had wished would never come to be
I am falling hesitantly away from you…a distance I have never known
The gift I gave from my Heart you refused to open…refused to see
The many years between us… this Love, as then I should have shown

No, I am not the same person you knew before…an unknown entity?
Perhaps…but I will follow my path yet not lucid…
to strengthen my stride
To rekindle my passion once more…to give of my Heart…to truly be
I have revealed all that I must…exposed my reason…nothing to hide

This last gift born from me…to instill always in you…
"Faith, Hope, Love"
These three simple words, if held true to your heart…
to endure all of time
Unmask for just one moment who you are…
from within…from above
Let the power of believing soothe you once more…once again sublime

My wish is that you believe…believe in who you are…
believe what you will be
For a time our paths may be uncertain…and if doubtful…look above
And should there be a time you feel abandoned…
too weary, too tired to see
Reach within to find that gift born from my heart…
to instill always in you…
…my "Faith, Hope, Love"

"Virtue"

*You were my every dream when all was lost
But the past refused our future…as such…our cost
The lies could never place to rest the hurt that lay within
Our choice would be our ending…to never again begin*

*Obstinate is the heart when so many would deceive
The promise of what could be…but who do we believe?
No, I am not like the others…my Love is always true
In time you will believe again…if only now you knew?*

*My youth it now denies me…I am all I choose to be
I am not of what I was before…not what some wish to foresee
My measure is my patience…none will move my stance
Never to be invalid of Love again…never to risk nor chance*

*For those that seize without devotion…to them I must deny
Lies, deception, vanquished promises…on these I cannot rely
Read between the lines of desire…the disparity…know what is true
Don't let words lacking meaning…leave you troubled and blue*

*May patience be our guide…may patience be our "Virtue"
For those that choose deceit…may they never mystify you?
I am only but one being…my life in truth I will find my way
My Body and Soul for only one…my heart it shall never stray*

"The Ring"

For so many years it lay tarnished…latent…cold
Forsaken by the many vanquished dreams…far too long
He ponders, reaches for it…his Love…to once again hold
It shimmers with life at his touch…why…so right…so wrong?

He wanted so very much to wear again, its trust…all its glory
Would defiance and regret abandon his hopes of what should be?
How many times did he covet and try…try to say "I am Sorry"
Would they be given the chance, again once more…to finally see?

He caresses it…besieged by his Love…his one, his only desire
Only as two could they share it…it is weak, frail, nothing without her
To feel its warmth and comfort once more…like embers to a fire
Dare he place it on his hand yet again…bewildered…unsure?

If only they knew the path that lay before them…their destined call?
To never fear loneliness…no sadness…to feel again their denied Love
Unified by the entity of "The Ring"…to stand strong…to never fall
To wish for what was promised from vows before…a gift from above

He looks at its brilliance once more, a pledge,
his promise to never let it go
The time is not now as he longs for her words…the joy it would bring
He places it once more, next to his Heart…
only awaiting time, to finally know
His years, His Life…His Love always remains…
none could compare…
"The Ring"

"Believe"

Once again I am at the Cross Roads
As in many times before…the path of least resistance
But always…no matter the distance of my Heart
It is always you I am destined to return to

So many times I have tried to free this Heart
The many who have tried…to win it from you
It is not theirs to have, to win, to take
And as my path always true to you…so is my Heart

I am patient in wishing and believing it is you
You that will once again "Believe" in who I am
As we near our "Silver" milestone…I am here
Awaiting the words I have so longed to hear

I cannot guide your Hand or Heart…it is only you
Reach out and take what has never been given
My Heart and my Hand has always been yours
Reach inside and you will find it there… "Believe"

"The Ending"

I had wished for more…a life time…you and I
But the Winds of Change took you away
No, I cannot return to what was my dream
To accept and move onward…tomorrow…another day

For all of these years it was only you…always you
My hopes and wishes…to follow, to build our dream
My Life…now the better part spent…I am tired
And again, I will awaken to tomorrow…and you not there

Time will help subside what I feel deep inside for you
And yes, your memory…always in my Heart, my Soul
I will carry it…never to forget…but always to remember
The good…the bad…but so worth the journey

Would I change what was??...Not a moment
Would I change what could be??...I cannot…only we can
What is written is done…no remorse…forward
Let this "The Ending"…be our beginning

"Not A Day Goes By"

*As I look around me…it seems that everything reminds me
Reminds me of you…how we were…what we used to be
The sunset at night…like the fire red of your hair
The gentle morning breeze…the subtle scent of you there*

*The warmth of the midday Sun…thoughts of lying next to you
The innocence of a child's laughter…like yours…so carefree…true
The softness of a newborn's skin…like your caress, your touch
Our many moments together…these moments I miss so much*

*There is nothing I would not do…not a place I would not go
To turn back the hands of time…this and more I want you to know
To give you all that you deserve in your life…my hope…to truly try
Not a moment in time I'll not think of you… "Not A Day Goes By"*

"Where I Belong"

It is in my sense of urgency that I feel drawn toward you
The dormancy I had felt for so long…now awake…so new
Is it my Heart and Soul calling out to yours…can it truly be?
Has it been so long since Love was dismissed…to lastly see?

As I look toward you…there is a passion like never before
I aspire to be with you…to hold you…to touch you for evermore
To weave our hopes and dreams into ones we can never deny
To overcome our hatred…our pain…no barriers should we try

I stand before you…I pledge my devotion…my oath of true Love
In the times I questioned this Heart and Soul…this time from above
It is a gift from those beyond…those that see what we refuse to
No longer can I sit without a voice…to veil what I always knew

I will not be silenced any longer…I cannot control this Love that I feel
Elation beyond all I have known…not an illusion, but what I deem real
If this my only chance to be whole once more…I will wait…I will be
To be all that you could ever ask…to desire…to set your heart free

Allow me this time once more…you will never be alone…I am here
My Love…my compassion for you…always beside you…always near
In times of uncertainty…the questions…this time I won't be wrong
No longer set adrift in a sea of confusion…you are "Where I Belong"

"Tomorrow May Never Come"

Shallow is the one that does not share their heart
For they only have one
Dream for today and share for tomorrow
As that dream may never return

Tears may flow from joy or sadness
Don't hide them, but share them
What we see, breathe and touch
Seize the moment…if only for one second

Be it love or anger in your heart
Release it, let it be free
Do not promise time you cannot keep or share
Live, Love and Laugh like there is no tomorrow

Life is too precious…it can never be bought
But of all of these…remember
"Tomorrow May Never Come"

"Warmth"

I often watched you from a distance…unsure…afraid to speak
The "Warmth" within you I could feel…a feeling...one never known
I wished to know you, my avenged reluctance and manner weak
My apprehension and untimely demise…if only I could have shown

My intent not of desire…but one besieged to deepened curiosity
Why? To doubt this allure stronger than a need…I must declare
A chance to know you…to learn your "Warmth"…when would it be?
Casual…my attempts to see you…my path always to find you there

How time would encourage our friendship…
driven…our passion to survive
If only we had found sooner this "Warmth"…our destiny of decline?
Parallel our pasts…soon bring about our meaning…
in haste we revive
All is never lost should we build into tomorrow…
it is ours…ours to refine

Believe in providence…patience in our chosen paths…soon to convene
It is the "Warmth" that draws us nearer…
no longer latent, no longer cold
Time honors those who wait…renews what was once refused…unseen
Our friendship of trust…our meaning…
beyond any gifts we can behold

… "Warmth"

"Live Life…Let Live"

The morning air is chilled…wrapped in a long winter's proclivity
Soon to breathe new life…breeding new hopes and expectations
Nature again calls upon the earth to herald immaculate delivery
A time to bid farewell, a parting to yesterday…
to bring about revelations

It seems like a lifetime…the many days surrendered
to cold and darkness
The warmth and light of the day contests and rebels…
"stay no longer"
I return to lay my claim…to diminish all bereavement…
a time to progress
"Live Life…Let Live"… simplistic words…yet in time will grow ever
stronger

The unborn, the seedlings that were once quiescent…
await their calling
Bonds of Love study regeneration…
a time to warm ailed hearts…to grow
Of Love that could not mend…
which excused novel warmth…their falling?
Sadness trickles from the crevices of invalid realization…
a time to let go

"Live Life…Let Live"…
tides of Love and Faith will nourish the seeds of all
The cold and darkness will not linger much longer…
instill faith in tomorrow
Nurture the unborn…the seedlings…
the love and life thought beyond our call
Yesterday is only but a memory…"Live Life…Let Live"…
bid farewell to sorrow

"Blessed"

The ground glistens…it is a blanket of purity…
Angel soft…Cloud white
The birth of yet another season…a time of rest…renewal…tranquility
Driven by the deepest depths of my Heart…wishing all will be so right
A haven of new Love prospers…a need to reach out…to foster serenity

Our life at times full of ridicule…scorn…
forever searching for our reason
I am "Blessed" in knowing that I have all and more…
I am humbled…grateful
I have Love…I feel Love…I give Love…always…
not just of this one season
No, our World is not that of flawlessness…
but it is ours to make bountiful

Should tomorrow not be mine…
I will depart with no misgivings…no sorrow
My blessings lay within my family…my friends…
my World of endless pride
A gift that is not of material…but one I can never buy…
one I can never borrow
The gift of Love, Peace…Serenity…one that lays within…
one held deep inside
I am…"Blessed"

"Tomorrow"

How often you would run away…
to hide from a world you desired behind
The confines of your room were your mask to defend and confess to all
To seek answers…to inspire dreams…
but only loneliness you would find
A choice solitary in your quest for truth…
I watched in angst…I watched you fall

So many times I waited your calling…
but the past would replicate…deny me
My strength could no longer build our constitution…
to unearth the last void
Tears of anger and hurt…I had to refuse you…
afraid…my choice to let you be
Could it be our journey had reached its end…
was all we shared destroyed?

A journey devised from an astute yet willful past…
we would honor no prosperity
To share our humbling pleasures,
none could equal our secluded jubilation
To wish and want for more…
would it be to hunger or a need innate in voracity?
Beyond today there is always "Tomorrow"…
Believe…it will be your exultation

I have no answers to what lies before us…
I will convalesce…I sit in silence
Perhaps time will be caring…
to consent us the chance to be whole…destiny?
The warmth from this my heart…
it will always be near you, yours in dependence
Find the truth…it is there…fear not "Tomorrow" …
"Tomorrow" will set you free

"Forgiveness"

Too many years living with the past…the reminder of his sadness
Taunted by his tangled heart…confused, lost, oblivious to remorse
He questions each day…why…how to forget…to seek Forgiveness?
Ordained to silence…his heart at rest…callus, cold…with no recourse

So easy to weave such a web of deception…to banish what lays within
The sorrow he carries as each minute passes…
to leisurely weaken his Soul
His hopes that all soon will pass…awaken this death…
his life would begin
To believe in what was once shared…to reunite in the present…
to be whole

To live in a World without a need to seek vengeance…to chastise Love
Again, he asks why…
how could he dawn the clothes he could never wear?
To reach within…to reach out…
to hold, to nurture…beyond and above
How long will she linger…
to become a path of no return…to never care?

He reaches within…his torment climaxed…
he pleads "I must Love again"
To believe in oneself…to Love who and what we are…this his answer?
His past must once again become his present…his future…no disdain
To not reside on what was lost, but learned through Love…
to forgive her

Too many years living with the past…
now his present…no longer sadness
He reaches out for her hand…his Heart and Soul
resurrected…"Forgiveness"

"Silence Is Not A Sound"

*We have dreamed…we have shared…we were all that we chose to be
Our time…our patience…was it lost…surrendered…never to be found?
We perceived our happiness…our hopes now elusive for our eyes to see?
Contempt of each other…to remind us always…"Silence Is Not A Sound"*

*To believe that all will be right…perhaps soon…perhaps never?
In distance I am near you…in imminence I am far…shall I wait?
Never a memory until time has passed us by…to embrace it forever?
The answers…not ours this time…our future erodes, our dire strait?*

*We will be…it is in our strengths to be all that we can be…to be more
Let our pasts not become our future again…to believe in what is sincere
To find love within ourselves once more…it is the key that opens the door
The door that leads us to tomorrow…hold no sorrow…to abandon all fear*

*We have dreamed…we have shared…we were all that we chose to be
Our time…our patience…was it lost…surrendered…never found?
We perceived our happiness…our hopes now elusive for our eyes to see?
Contempt of each other…to remind us always…"Silence Is Not A Sound"*

"My Best Friend"
(02-05-1962)

From the moment we met…I knew
It was "You", "You" who touched me deep within
The one I could trust and confide in…"You"
The one without ending…you taught from where to begin

Some would say "An Angel, a Miracle…Heaven Sent"
All of that and more…steadfast…a blessing
Not one in my life to near compare…to compliment
To compliment my Heart…my reason for being

You have become my guide, my dreams…my reason
To allow me the freedom…to be who I am without end
To accept and love my imperfections…to be the only one
I am beyond elation…so grateful that you are…
"My Best Friend"

"I Love You Always...Forever"

I have done my best to express and show my Love for you
I am not angered by your resentment...or to never return
I have no reason to be...your decision is heartfelt and true
My only hope is that we will not forget what was learned

The many years we strived to remain the best for each other
Our Children, our Joy, our Pride, our Love, our Sharing
You were all that wasn't possible at times...a Best Friend...a Mother
And most of all...your compassion...your love and constant caring

To go forward...begin a path...to be the best we can be
Not only for those we chance to meet...to share once more
But always for each other...let us not miss what we didn't see
Let us never be afraid...too seek what lies beyond the door

I will forever be in honor of having the time that we once knew
I can't imagine not ever having the Love that we shared...never
There will always be a part of you in me...and hopefully me in you
And should tomorrow not be ours... "I Love
You...Always...Forever"

Why Did You Hurt Me?

Was I right to leave when my time stood still
void in my sense of direction?
Grasping for a dream once thought believable…
possible…one held so dear
I wished no hurt upon you…or to those we love…
my intent was only absolution
I wanted only to be all that I could…not the enemy you had devised
out of fear

My choices…that of a "Dying Soul"…
to ask forgiveness…to seek solace…silence
I wished for no other to be at my side…
I asked of you the same…my only plea
My heart exposed…vulnerable…
only to be trampled…ravaged by lame defiance
Was it to avenge your pain…to seek justice from anger…

Why Did You Hurt Me?
To relinquish the trust we promised sacred…
only to become enchanted by lust
To never seek out what is truth…to refute our efforts…
to be what we were not
Why did you let "him" in…
did you reach out to encourage discord and not trust?
I am again broken…my demeanor weakened,
weary beyond any hope…distraught

I will accept and conquer the distance you wished for…
to again stand with pride
To begin the Journey I once thought traveled…the one of hope…
to set us "Free"
I will rise above what soon becomes my memory…
and still my Love…I will not hide
In time this Journey will meet its end…and still I will ask…
Why Did You Hurt Me?

"If Only You Knew"
"Happy Birthday Cindy"

I reminisce thru the many years. . .in jubilation. . .I have watched you grow
Time nurtured your roots. . .exposing you...to become all that you would be
An offering of elusive beauty that none could compare. . .any could bestow
None could possess this beautiful and delicate flower. . .so soon to grow free

My years of delight in your presence. . .your grace. . .to shelter. . .to hold you
"If Only You Knew". . .If only you could see what I had seen. . .what I could feel
Your place forever fixed in my heart. . .never to fade. . .always sacred, always true
No, not for one moment can I not think of you. . .my Love, it is surreal

How one day I would carelessly let you go. . .only to regret what I had done
Accepting I could no longer nourish what only in time would soon convey
Stolen from my ground. . .you would seek new light. . .seek another's Sun
My life never again the same. . .no, not without you. . .never another day

Show me the light that you seek. . .honor my Love. . .this Love you once knew
"If Only You Knew". . .the emptiness in this Heart. . .without you all is amiss
My light would again warm you. . .my tears of enchantment would sustain you
Again renewed. . .our future. . .never our broken past would we reminisce

If our time is now only in memories. . .I will try to believe. . .I will try to under-stand
Perhaps another time will come, may our Love until then linger strong and true
I will dream of you beside me. . .to dream that you will again take my hand
My Heart. . .my Love always Sacred...always True. . . "If Only You Knew"
. . . "If Only You Knew"

"Souls...Forever Lost"

He gazes deeply into her distant and abandoned eyes
He remembers a time when they seldom cried or shed a tear
He was once her delight...her happiness...the sparkle she now denies
Windows they say to our Souls...hers timid, now led astray in fear?

Her fears of losing all she ever wanted and desired...is it now lost?
Would she sell her Soul devoid of Heart...in prejudice, without thought?
If so...what lies in her future...without a dream...at what cost?
A Soul once surrendered...never again returns, it can never be bought

He wishes he could have salvaged her Soul and Spirit...too give life
What is a body without one's Soul...broken...again, too never be?
If only he could cleanse and renew her Spirit...too banish her strife
Did her suffering and pain blind her sight...would she ever see?

He feels the emptiness in her heart...how could he have let it subside?
Why was time so merciless to not let him see sooner, too find the answer?
So many times his past would deny her of Love, the many years he would hide
His only wish now...too be all that she needs...too forever remain beside her

Latent is his journey...he reaches out one last time to touch her hand
It is cold and annulled of emotion...his loss beyond any darkness...his demise
He will always remember the days he had strived to take his one last stand
Too be all that he could be once more...he accepts his loss...yet he still denies

He gazes deeply into her distant and abandoned eyes
He remembers a time when they seldom cried or shed a tear
He was once her delight...her happiness...the sparkle she since denies
Windows they say to our Souls...Forever Lost, forever in fear...

"Our Journey"

As each hour has passed…like my Love it now wanes from what is lost
I must abandon this place…
if my choice be my destiny…it is solely at my cost
No longer yours to hold any burden…
I will seek out my future...my dream
My past is no longer the present…
no…I am much more…not what I seem

I have battled this moment for what I feel a life time…
I am no longer fearful
I can no longer deny those who need me…
too share…too love…too be whole
I journeyed far and beyond with this heart and mind…
but in absence of my Spirit
I am troubled by many paths I have taken…
but perseverance and pride my true grit

My heart steadfast and true…
a place always there for you…it will always be
I have looked beyond, deep inside for absolution…
uncovered for all who wished to see
I have forgave all who were unjust…
my heart and conscience with no more sorrow
It was as in mine…their choice to steer destiny…
to go before, to find tomorrow

Should I return…it will be at your calling…
it is your voice and message I will hear
I will be deaf and silent to those who wish to stray me…
but never to those dear
I must go now…I must prepare for a World
I have at times only wished to forget
To once again find my place…a solace rich in Love…
to choose with no regret

The present now becomes our past…as each hour lingers…
we are our future
A future that lies in hopes of today, tomorrow…
to hold, to coddle…to nurture
May our Souls and Spirits always remain at peace…
to hearten "Our Journey"
To accept all that we cannot change…
to welcome what we can and choose to be

"Loving You"

"Loving You" has not been easy
For this troubled heart and mind
Smothered by self doubts and darkness
Searching, wishing and hoping to find

Someone like you or similar
To think of what I may have left behind
To daily renounce the truth within
How could I have been so blind?

I will not return to the places I have been
Nor will I wish that day…to wish that memory
But for truth I will walk beside you
It is only with you I have longed to be

Though distance may be between us
Not a day I will not think of you
It is you that has made me whole once more
It is for you that my Heart stands true

I will promise to Love you dearly
With all this my heart can bestow
I will Love you as every second passes
So from "Just Me"…I wished you to know

"Hope"

You captured my Soul, you bordered my Heart
You gave me "Hope" when times were distant and apart
When lost and unsure, no place to hide or run
My path was long yet clear, you were the only one

My day becomes inclusive…as I think of only you
So much I've left to say, so much I've left to do
If we are just a beginning, my wish without an end
Broken pasts…only but a memory…if we allow to mend

My gift is very simple; I choose only and offer to you
To Love, honor and protect you, perhaps one day "I do"
No more fears will haunt us; one less tear will be shed
My love with one condition, no joy or pain remains unsaid

My Heart and Soul is yours, should you accept or choose
I will Love you with conviction, this feeling I will not lose
I will give to you my Spirit; let me love you by the sea
Let me fill you with the tides of "Hope";
let us be who we can be

"The Harbor"

*As I peer towards the clear blue skies…it is Heaven that I see
All my grieving subsides…all is calm knowing that your arms await me
You have been my lifeboat…my anchor when storms were cast
The Harbor that holds my Love forever…the one that heals my past*

*You have been my guide when these eyes too tired…legs too weak
You released me from my silence…my voice when I could not speak
How do I ever rescind my lifelong debt…I am forever lost without you?
I have nothing but my Love to give…my body is old but my heart is true*

*It is my love that at times will wane…but always returns…ever stronger
My body, my Spirit spellbound by you…my Soul forever yours and longer
Never to abandon your side…in distance I will carry you always in my heart
Knowing soon…may Godspeed my deliverance…never again a moment apart*

*As I peer towards the clear blue skies…it is Heaven that I see
All my grieving subsides…all is calm knowing that your arms await me
You have been my lifeboat…my anchor when storms were cast
The Harbor that holds my Love forever…the one that heals my past*

"Papillion"

I sit alone...again, this darkened room consumes me
A choice that I wonder...was it truly mine?
Mine to make...from beyond...a message I was futile to see?
A gift or a curse...her message...is it a sign?

Emotionally I feel drained...but yet again...reborn
To grow again Spiritually...to again Love who I am
A wrath of feelings...I feel dragged, tormented and torn
My only wish is all subsides...soon...soon I hope...damned

At times...I feel like I could cry a lake of tears
My stubbornness and need for self control allows me to exist
This Heart and Soul hungers for Love to overcome all fears
To open the doors and windows...to breathe again and not resist

I will emerge from this darkened room...no, not alone
To Love who I am...my Family...my Life...to Love deeply
To be all that I can be...to soar so freely... "Papillion"
My hand shaken as I pen my Heart and Soul...my reason to Be?

"Unified"

There is a quiet…a silence…a solitude…is this now my inner peace?
Is it the calm before the storm…a prelude to a quandary of confusion?
Am I only a fool to believe that this is of my own accord…
my own release?
Is it that I have accepted your absence…
your memory now my delusion?

This feeling of warmth…such calming…
no longer the fear of being solitary
I pray to those above who have conferred this gift…do not abandon me
I have endured this pain for far too long…
my promise to never again bury
I cannot return to where I have been…
I am weary…too weak to again be

I have given all that I could…I have been all that I was chosen to be
I must conclude this chapter…
lay down this book of secrets…I rest…I wait
Allow me to go forward once more…
lead me to the path I must now see
I will go now should you grant me that wish…
I will not stray…nor hesitate

This silence…this solitude I have delayed for so long…
perhaps it is real?
A sentiment naively discouraged…
I longed thru years of distraught…mystified?
I am ready…I have returned to where I always belonged…
I can again see…feel
I bid my farewell…I caress my past one last time…
this Heart…this Soul
…"Unified"

"Falling Away"

Time has passed us by so quickly…much faster than I once thought
The love we thought could linger on…
now fading…falling…"Falling Away"
I tried to capture your charade…yet such illusion could not be sought
Our world void…retired existence…
stealth our cause born a life in dismay

We would seek freedom from our past…
yet I could never abandon you
In a moment you were gone…
seeking the life you had longed forever
Impatient as it would seem…
I would sadly honor your wish…had I knew
My wish to Love you…to hurt or cause you harm…
my promise was "never"

"Falling Away"…y
our desire to leave me gathering my tears in silence
Sheltering exposed emotions…anger would not guide me nor lead me
Resent could not sway or affront my heart…
time would strengthen reliance
Had I finally found in you a truth obscured for so long…to finally see?

So many times I scavenged uncertainty…
yet the answers remained the same
My illusions that held me captive for so long…
now fervent to find my way
I will honor your wishes…
leave you your freedom you so desire to tame
In time we may regret our reasons…
I will not return…I am "Falling Away"

"The Light"

You have a profound effect and nuance to this sometimes troubled mind
The years you have been near, yet far…
beside me…never a moment behind
You often sat in silence…awaiting my pleas for guidance…
my fated call
To unearth the darkness…the indefinite…
to bring about truths for all

For decades you were passed on…
from one to another…a Spirit's marathon
I did not know you at first…
but time would reveal your reason…your passion
I am grateful that I found you…always without
condition…always there
"The Light" of Day… "The Light" of Night…
"The Light" of Love…you share

"The Light" that emits from beyond all boundaries…
a beacon to behold
My journey would become merciless…
without warning, my future untold
I have been bequeathed to tell others of your presence…
your immensity
To not fear you…but to receive your gift…
the gift to conquer all adversity

The Life and Love that you breathe into all that seek
solace…inner peace
May "The Light" you bring always prevail over darkness…
to never cease
I will believe in you…
in time as each kindred Spirit becomes "The Light"
To never deny your Love, your warmth…
your truths…never from my Sight…

You will always remain… "The Light"

"Timeless"

What would time be if it seized no limitations…no policy?
Would it stand still for the moments we hold so precious and dear?
Would it become still in times of regret…in times of despondency?
"Timeless"…when euphoria thrives…yet it is the incongruent we fear

A world of inequity…to some only black…to others only white
To each our option of only one reserved emotion…to love or to hate?
To divide our emotional realm on such absurd thought…our plight?
"Timeless"…when the bizarre becomes our reality…
our individual fate

If life is "Timeless"…do we seek the eternal…to not grow or to study?
To never leave the womb…to become ageless…latent in our passage
Does smugness become staunch with denial…to seek no proclivity?
The many moments I have pondered my life "Timeless"…
my selfish mirage

If I am culpable of such egocentric desires at times…do absolve me
But am I alone in these my moments of persuasion? …
My mind is restless
An old expression troubles me…
"watch what you wish for"… can it be?
Could life become captive to the everlasting…
the question remains…
"Timeless"

"A Perfect Storm"

Dark clouds loom ominously in the distance…in approach of their prolonged passion
The air is damp, intense…steadfast with revival…evermore disposed now to respond
Provisional Nuptials of two empowered elements…assembling their wrath in communion
What is forthcoming is not to be reviled…but must be venerated from the beyond

To bring forth healing to all once lame…cleansing wounds absent of thoughtfulness
The impurities of the World will soon bow in a weakened state…imploring remorse
Winds of change will bring about warmth and new breath to those chilled and relentless
Tides of the highest seas will erode and immerse the many uncensored…no recourse

Peace will reside once more…no more tears will be shed in angst…but only in harmony
Laughter will be heard across the vastness of our lands…this offering from our Heaven
The freedom to express what is natural from the Heart…unborn Souls prevail in Calvary
Bring about these four winds of change…the cleansing Seas that number in Seven…
Make haste…make welcome…"The Perfect Storm"

"Words"

It is a dark yet delicate abyss where I choose to be resident to now
Please do not fear for me...please do not presume my altered state
I must passage onward...to find closure...my final curtain, my final bow
I can no longer delight in the unknown I have since prolonged to hate

Many have carried me this far...this new independence now provokes me
Sing no overtures nor pleas for me...I am much stronger in my daring
Those that gave so liberally of their wisdom...I revere them graciously
Those that isolated my Soul from endless storms...I eulogize their caring

The balance between the sullen and jovial is like that of a fine silken strand
Never contradict its frailty...but weave passion into an attire of infinite pride
To share it without prejudice...to share it in "Words" that all will understand
If devoid of my hopes and dreams...is there relevance?...Only we can decide

To seek renewal, to foster what is righteous in our hearts...let it be profound
Spartan is the hand that pens thoughtlessness and makes it seem forthright
Believe in a new light where darkness has ruled...protest where once no sound
A voice is the dominion to raze or recreate...learn from the day...lead into the night
...give reverence to the right...to the influence of "Words"

Table of Contents

Table of Contents

Table of Contents

Printed in the United States
134262LV00001B/38/P